ROOM BY ROOM
DESIGNSOURCE

ROOM BY ROOM DESIGNSOURCE

ALEJANDRO BAHAMÓN

COLLINS DESIGN
An Imprint of HarperCollinsPublishers

ROOM BY ROOM DESIGNSOURCE

First Edition published in 2006 by:
Collins Design
An Imprint of HarperCollins*Publishers*
10 East 53ʳᵈ Street
New York, NY 10022
Tel: (212) 207-7000
Fax: (212) 207-7654
collinsdesign@harpercollins.com
www.harpercollins.com

Distributed throughout the world by:
HarperCollins*Publishers*
10 East 53ʳᵈ Street
New York, NY 10022
Fax: (212) 207-7654

Packaged by
LOFT Publications
Via Laietana, 32 4.° Of. 92
08003 Barcelona, Spain
Tel: +34 932 688 088
Fax: +34 932 687 073
loft@loftpublications.com
www.loftpublications.com

Editor:
Alejandro Bahamón

Translation:
Heather Bagott

Art Director:
Mireia Casanovas Soley

Layout:
Luis F. Sierra

Library of Congress Cataloging-in-Publication Data

Bahamón, Alejandro
Room by room designsource / Alejandro Bahamón
       p. cm.
  ISBN-13: 978-0-06-113893-5 (trade pbk.)
  ISBN-10: 0-06-113893-2 (trade pbk.)
 1. Interior decoration.   I. Title. II. Title: Room by room designsource.
  NK2115.B24 2006
  747—dc22
                                          2006018430

Printed in Spain
First Printing, 2006

Contents

The design of residential spaces evolves constantly and always offers novel and useful solutions for architects and designers, as well as for owners and users in general. The evolution of the building industry has driven the development of innumerable techniques and materials with which to build a house. Although architects continue to use traditional building materials such as wood, stone, or metal, nowadays the range of possibilities has been greatly increased thanks to the latest technology. Glass in all of its forms, thin metal sheets used for paneling, plastic materials, and pieces made from recycled materials are just some of the components that serve to enrich the contemporary house. Today, character is breathed into each of the spaces of a house through a series of technical details and finishes, as well as through the use of the space itself, bestowing a very specific style on each of the rooms.

Likewise, the latest trends in furniture, lighting, and decoration help to define a new way in which to approach the design of today's house. The selection of projects designed by some of the most internationally renowned architects and designers make *Room by Room DesignSource* a fountain of inspiration for any reader interested in residential design. Its classification, as a guided tour around each one of the rooms of a house, converts this book into a practical and easy-to-use guide. Each chapter presents a wide variety of styles, materials, and finishes that serve as reference points when deciding on the design of each space.

Entrances

The first stop in this tour around all of the spaces of a house is the entrance. This is the place where we are received, the point of separation between public and private, and the place from where we are invited into the interior world of a house. From the outside, depending on the requirements of each project, entrances can be perceived as considerably significant statements, inviting the visitor in, or as subtle, barely perceptible elements that are integrated within the housing of the building or are hidden behind walls or natural screens. Inside, the entrance hall is directly related to the circulation zones of the house, giving these spaces a great dynamism and enabling them to assume a wide range of shapes and dimensions. Entrances can vary from spaces with high ceilings where verticality reigns by virtue of the siting of the stairwell, as in multilevel houses, to long corridors where the horizontal component predominates.

The entrance is the presentation space of the house and usually the element that links the rest of the rooms, which is why architects and designers take great care in its configuration. From here, the workings of the project should be understood, inviting the visitor to the most social areas of the house, such as the living room and dining room, and also controlling the access to the more private areas, like the bedrooms. Due to the transitional nature of entrances, they are usually spaces with little furniture, thus giving greater importance to the materials and architectural elements. Natural light and artificial lighting can help merge the entrance with the rest of the spaces of the house or contribute to emphasize its contrast. Zenithal light, where possible, is characteristic of this type of space, given that such lighting cannot be easily used in other places in the house. This feature emphasizes the transitory character of the entrance, which is often perceived as a kind of an interior courtyard.

© Undine Pröhl

The glass walls, completely independent from the system of metallic beams and columns, creates a delicate image and gives this entrance the air of a balcony overlooking a yard.

The need for an elevator allows for the creation of a tall glass box next to the stairwell, which enriches this space of vertical proportions.

© Jordi Miralles

15

© Eugeni Pons

16

The hall and the circulation areas have been defined by way of the red floor covering, as if it were a carpet leading the visitor to the rest of the rooms.

19

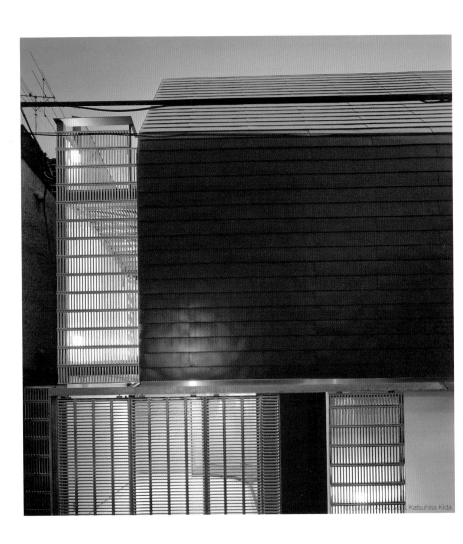

© Katsuhisa Kida

© Satushi Asakawa & Katsuhisa Kida

© Elisabeth Felicella

The wall that provides access to this house has been designed as a large window so as to enjoy the view of the yard from the living room, which is directly opposite the entrance.

© Jordi Miralles

© Jordi Miralles

© Pep Escoda

© Kouji Okatomo

The two levels of this apartment have been used to create a split-level hall that serves as a way to distribute the different zones of the project.

© Jordi Miralles

31

© Eugeni Pons

The stairwell, built in double sheet metal, just in front of the glass access façade, opens up the views of the far end of the space and also lets light into the garage.

© Makoto Yoshida

© Makoto Yoshida

© Makoto Yoshida

© Undine Pröhl

The sizable metallic panels make for a subtle and imperceptible access when closed, or a large and striking access when opened.

© Undine Pröhl

39

© Jordi Miralles

© Jordi Miralles

41

The indirect lighting highlights the interesting positioning of wooden panels that serve to define the entrance and the spaces of circulation of this apartment.

© Miquel Tres

The austerity of the shapes and
materials of this entrance hall
further enhances the impressive
view of the swimming pool and
exterior surroundings.

© Miquel Tres

© Hannes Henz

© Hannes Henz

© Tim Griffith

The zenithal light is reflected onto the stairwell, highlighting the sinuous shapes of this space and creating a visual effect that makes a trip upstairs rather inviting.

© Ignacio Martínez

Ignacio Martínez

Ignacio Martínez

© Eugeni Pons

The yard area preceding the entrance door can be designed as an outdoor room that serves as a preamble to the interior of the house.

3200
Ocean Drive

© Weldon Brewster

59

61

© Ignacio Martínez

© Ignacio Martínez

A red shape highlights the character of the access hall of this house, as well as serving as an articulating element leading to the circulation zones of the house.

© Andreas Greber

© Trevor Mein

© Shania Shegedyn

The entrance to this tropical country retreat features an outdoor courtyard, which houses a pond and large concrete paving stones.

© Eduardo Consuegra

© Luigi Filetici

© Kouji Okatomo

© Jordi Miralles

© Jordi Miralles

© Jordi Miralles

Living Rooms

The functions given to the living room space are as diverse as the styles and layouts that can be achieved, ranging from somewhere for large social gatherings to an intimate and personal space for relaxation or reading. The formality that has traditionally characterized this part of the house has given way to a fresher, more laid-back and avant-garde style over recent years. In this way a more personal atmosphere is created, adapting to the needs of each user. Innovative pieces of design and cutting-edge technologies can be incorporated, such as a home cinema or other technological equipment, which have revolutionized the layout and the shapes of furniture typical of this area. Depending on how this area of the house is planned, the living room space can be further adjusted to supply a wide variety of needs.

The architectural characteristics of a living room depend on various factors, such as the type of client, the structure of the building, or the project's program of activities. Unless the climate and conditions of the project dictate otherwise, this space should be west facing, as it is primarily frequented in the afternoons or early evening. High ceilings make for an impressive and fresh atmosphere, whereas a low roof creates a more cozy and intimate space. Warm materials such as wood, brick, or natural stone are the norm for this area. The furniture and decoration should emphasize the architectural character of the space, creating a uniform and harmonious atmosphere. This can be achieved by mixing furniture of varying styles, from rustic to avant-garde, enabling each corner of the living room to have its own identity.

The color green, which enhances the walls, certain furniture, and various decorative elements, serves as a unifying element between the different ambiences of this living room.

© Studio Arthur de Mattos Casas

83

© Matteo Piazza

The sobriety of the space, achieved with minimal architectural elements and very gentle shades, serves as an ideal frame for the designer furniture contained herein.

© Matteo Piazza

© Matteo Piazza

© Jordi Miralles

© Jordi Miralles

© Jordi Miralles

87

© Luis Ros

The cushions in this living room resemble pieces of a jigsaw puzzle that can be arranged into numerous configurations, creating a flexible space suitable for a wide variety of uses.

© Jordi Miralles

© Roberto Pierucci, Sonia Cocozza

The two floors of this house were conjoined in order to create a very high space, where the living room is linked to the bedroom area above.

© Roberto Pierucci, Sonia Cocozza

© Pedro Mahamud

© Pedro Maharnud

99

© Adam Buttler

The rich texture of the bricked
arched ceiling of this space
is a decorative element in itself,
bringing warmth and personality
to the living room area.

© Adam Buttler

© Adam Buttler

© Adam Buttler

© Ricardo Labougle, Ana Cardinale

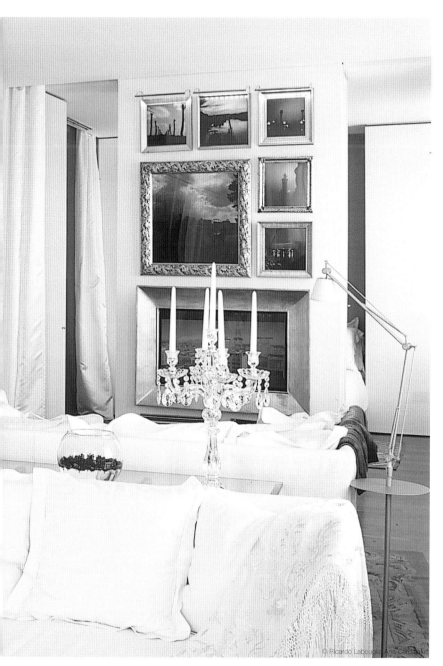

In this living space diverse styles have been brought together, from the rustic original structure and the cow skin rug to the brightly colored polyurethane furniture.

© Roberto Pierucci, Donatella Bernabò

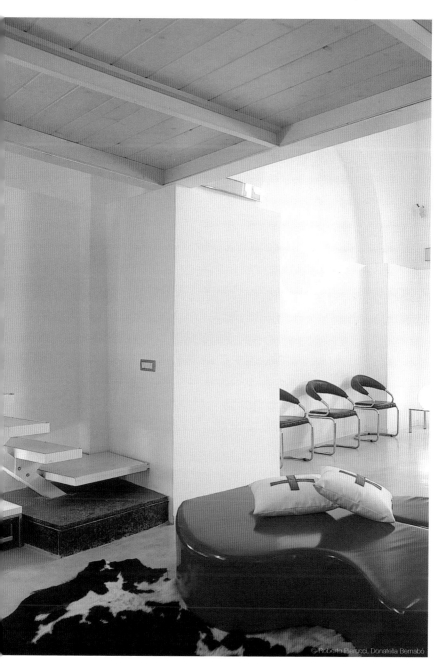

© Roberto Pierucci, Donatella Bernabò

© Conrad White

Loft-type buildings allow for
a fluid space where various
ambiences can be created,
playing on the layout of the
furniture and dividing panels.

115

© Matteo Piazza

117

Highly resistant materials and finishes, which characterize industrial spaces, can be transformed into interesting elements in loft conversions.

© Elizabeth Felicella

© Paul Warchol

© Michael Moran

© Michael Moran

© Paul Warchol

© Ignacio Martinez

■ The low ceiling generates an
intimate and cozy space in this
living room, contrasting well with
the zenithal light that flows in
from above the stairwell.

© Ignacio Martinez

© Ignacio Martínez

131

© Arnaldo Pappalardo

The living room of this house
has become a gallery that
opens up completely onto the
yard, thanks to the large-scale
sliding doors of the main façade.

© Arnaldo Pappalardo

133

© Undine Pröhl

© Eduardo Consuegra

© Eugeni Pons

© Paul Warcho[l]

© Paul Warchol

141

© Shania Shegedyr

The metallic chairs give a
delicate touch and can be easily
moved—ideal for apartments
and small spaces.

© Shania Shegedyn

© Shania Shegedyn

© Björg

Dining Rooms

The dining room is the heart of the home: the center of the family get-together par excellence and, in functional terms, the space that combines the social zone of the house with the service areas. Although not long ago it was preferable to have this room completely set away from the living room and kitchen, today it is a lot more common to find that the dining room is joined onto one or both of these zones. This open-plan style makes for an ample space that promotes daily family life together and allows social events to develop with greater ease and fluidity. According to the chosen design strategies, the link between the dining room and kitchen can be created in a more or less direct manner. Low walls, bar counters, sliding doors, or walls that hide part of the kitchen are some of the ways to partially differentiate these two spaces. On the other hand, a linking area between these two spaces and the dining room could even be used as a kitchen work surface.

The configuration of the dining room—its aspect, furniture, and lighting—plays a fundamental role in creating a functional and cozy space. Direct sunlight is best avoided, since it could prove troublesome at lunchtime, although the use of elements that filter the sunlight like curtains or blinds can always be incorporated. The proportions of this space vary according to the needs of the client and the size of the house, although generally it is housed within a smaller space than that of the living room. A longitudinal shape favors the use of a rectangular- or square-shaped table that can be extended when necessary. This shape of table works well when the dining area is an integral part of the kitchen. A round-shaped table accomodates a greater number of diners when space is limited. The lighting, which should be subtle in the whole area, should emanate from directly over the table, thus creating a cozy atmosphere in which the layout of the table is highlighted.

© Werner Huthmacher

For a small-sized independent space the most practical choice is a round table illuminated by a central ceiling lamp. The rug completes the whole effect.

© Jordi Miralles

© Jordi Miralles

© Jordi Miralles

© Jordi

The color white, which dominates the color scheme of the furniture in this dining room, contrasts well with the wooden floor and brick ceiling, creating a bright and luminous atmosphere.

© Jordi Miralles

© Jordi Miralle

© Jordi Miralles

© Jordi Miralles

A large-sized graphic illustration is the sole decorative element in this small dining room. The rectangular table attached to the wall optimizes the space.

© Eugeni Pons

© Jordi Miralles

175

The industrial aesthetic, inherited from the concept of loft conversions, serves to create a functional, flexible, and attractive dining room.

© Jordi Miralles

© Jordi Miralles

© Jordi Miralles

© Åke E:son Lindman

Although occupying a minimalist
space, this dining room achieves
coziness thanks to the use of wood:
in the table, the chairs, and the
paneling of one of the walls.

© Åke E:son Lindman

© Åke Eson Lindman

© Jordi Miralles

187

© Jordi Miralles

■ Inspiration has been drawn from
the industrial aesthetic in the
design of this small space, where
stainless steel and shades of gray
predominate.

© Jordi Miralles

© Jordi Miralles

© Jordi Miralles

© Åke Eison Lindman

© Graft

Low bar counters or high walls concealing the refrigerator are some of the practical design elements available when partially dividing the spaces of the dining room and kitchen.

195

© Graft

© Nuria Fuente

In this small space, the surface used as the dining room table can be converted into a work surface in the kitchen zone.

© Antonio Corcuer

© Antonio Corcuera

© Gogortza & Llorel

■ A simple object such as this translucent red plastic light is the decorative element that gives character to this dining room in a small apartment.

© Gogortza & Llorel

© Eugeni Pons

© Eugeni Po[

■ Wood—the predominant material in
this space, used in the floors, chairs,
and dividing panels—contrasts well
with the white to create a luminous
yet warm ambience.

© Jordi Miralles

© Jordi Miralle

© Jordi Miralles

215

© Åke Eison

© Åke E:son Lindman

© Jordi Miralles

© Jordi Miralles

© Joran Miralles

Although space is limited in this dining room, the contrast between white and black, along with decorative pieces in glass and metal, creates a formal and sophisticated whole.

221

© Eugeni Por

© Richard Lind

© Richard Lind

© Björg

The elegance of this dining room is achieved through the finishes, including the varnished wooden floor, the plywood paneling, and the furniture in shades of beige.

© Arnaldo Pappalar

The dining room of this house, within a large space with high ceilings, is defined by the pearl-gray-colored rug and the marble table in the same color.

© Tim Griffith

© Eugeni Pons

© Bruno Fröhl

233

© Jazek Kuz

The neutrality of an industrial space converted into a house lends itself to a wide range of possibilities for the dining room furniture, from rustic and industrial to modern and minimalist.

235

© Paul Warchol

237

© Jordi Miralle

239

© Jordi Miralles

Kitchens

The kitchen is the room of the house where the evolution in the functioning, technological advances, or style tendencies affecting the dwelling are reflected the most. Up until only a few decades ago the kitchen was a space reserved exclusively for the serving classes, whereas today it has become one of most important spaces for social reunions. This evolution has greatly affected its functioning and layout within the house. What was before an isolated room with the necessary minimum conditions of natural light and ventilation, and aesthetically conceived as a food-making laboratory, today has become a luminous place, integrated with the rest of the rooms of the home. In this way it is designed with the same functional principles and aesthetics as the rest of the house. It is simply another living space of the house, and in many cases is also used as a dining room or even as a work study.

The kitchen is the space in which the latest technological achievements can be found, such as cold- and heat-resistant materials; more powerful, smaller electrical appliances; or innovative materials that facilitate culinary tasks. Today, due to these advances, it is possible to design a fully fitted kitchen in a small walk-in space that disappears or appears as required. Its style can be as diverse as there are types of dwelling, clients, and functional necessities: rustic, modern, minimalist, small, or industrial. There is a wide range of possible finishes for the work surfaces, cupboards, and walls. The lighting here should be carefully thought out in order to create the appropriate work conditions, as well as a warm space that blends in well with the rest of the house.

© Eugeni Pon

In this small kitchen/dining room, white
marble has been used for the work
surfaces and dark wood for the table
and cupboards.

© Eugeni Pons

© Björg

© Björg

© Björg

The central island, which in this case serves as a work surface, divides the kitchen from the rest of the rooms in this loft-type dwelling.

© Jordi Miralles

253

© Matteo Piazza

© René Chavanne

© René Chavann

The design of this central piece of furniture, divided on two levels, serves to integrate the cooking zone with an auxiliary dining surface incorporated into the kitchen.

© René Chavann

© Eimar Cucine

© Elmar Cucin

© Nuria Fuentes

■ The red-colored high-density surface used as the work area of this kitchen also serves as a small dining area and decorative feature.

© Yael Pincus

© Yael Pincus

In this case, the dividing element between the kitchen and the rest of the space is an original, vertically styled wine rack that has been converted into a sculptural piece.

© Jordi Miralles

© Lewis Tsurumaki Lewis

The wooden and metal stairwell is fully integrated with the kitchen and, at the same time, serves as a dividing element that separates it from the other rooms of the house.

© Carlos Dominguez

An industrial aesthetic has been styled in the interior of this kitchen in a conventional apartment. The configuration of the kitchen is made up of stainless steel and wood modules.

© Elizabeth Felicella

283

© Adolf Bereut

Architecture, furniture, and kitchen equipment have been designed together in this space to achieve the desired uniform and durable look.

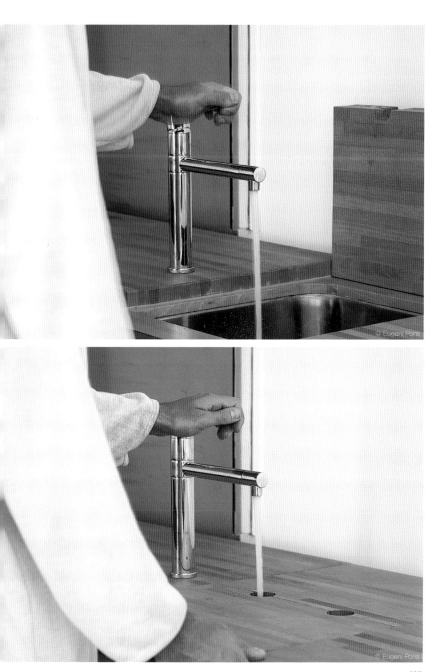

© Eugeni Pons

© Ricardo Labougle, Ana Cardini

The carved marble table and metal
chairs are key pieces in the design
of this elegant kitchen, where the
contrasts of color and material
elements predominate.

© Ricardo Labougle, Ana Cardinale

© Jordi Miralle

293

© Jordi Miralles

The scarcity of natural light in this space determined the predominant use of the color white, accentuated by the odd piece of red furniture.

© Jordi Miralles

This kitchen, situated in the middle of a loft dwelling, is unified with the rest of the space through the use of wood, present in all of the furniture, even in the refrigerator.

© Jordi Miralles

© Ignacio Martí

© Miquel Tr

© Ignacio Martinez

© Eduardo Consueg

A piece of furniture on wheels
accentuates the flexibility and
ampleness of the space, as well
as facilitating the taking of utensils
or food from the kitchen to the
dining room.

© Paul Warchol

© Paul Warchol

313

© Shanya Shegedyn

315

© Shanya Shegeo

319

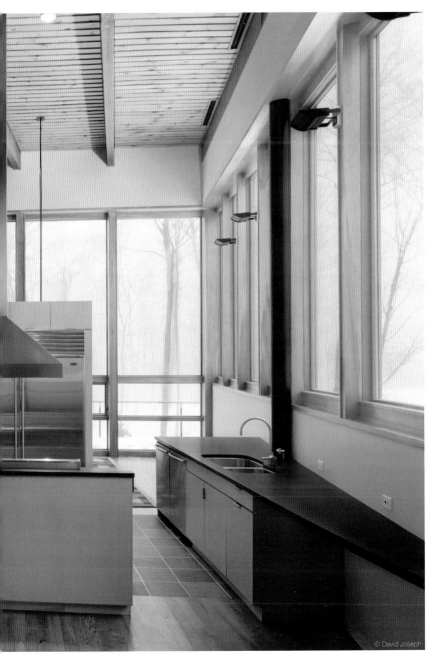

© David Joseph

Bedrooms

The bedroom is the place primarily reserved for relaxation and rest, and thus is the most private and intimate area of the house. The design of such spaces should favor these conditions and isolate this room as much as possible from the rest of the house and the exterior. Present-day thinking regarding these spaces is divided, however. While some designers emphasize formality and simplicity—with few distractions and an abundance of pure light and diaphanous textures—others, perhaps responding to size limitations or loft-type conversions, choose to integrate the bedroom fully with the rest of the spaces of the house. This can be achieved by way of sliding doors, wardrobe modules to divide two zones, or glass partitions. The lighting should be carefully controlled in the bedrooms to create a cozy and intimate atmosphere. In these spaces, direct light should be avoided; the flow of light needs to be controlled through architectural or decorative elements, such as blinds, screens, or curtains.

Furniture and decoration are determining factors when creating a space for relaxation, and should reflect the taste and needs of each client. Bedroom color schemes are normally based on soft tones, such as shades of gray, beige, and ochre, or calming bright shades of green or blue. While wood, a warm element, makes an ideal material for this type of space, a wide range of other suitable materials includes stone or brick for the wall and floor coverings, and metal and glass for the furniture. In larger houses, the bedroom may include a private reading or television room, whereas in smaller houses, a simple piece of furniture may suffice to highlight the bed and separate it from the rest of the space by way of thin curtains.

© Andrea Martiradon

The space housing the bed in this loft is created by a mezzanine, profiting from the double height of the space. The bedroom, although independent, is integrated with the rest of the dwelling.

© Tuca Reine

© Tuca Reinés

© Undine Pröhl

A small living area, a study, and a spacious bathroom have been added to this bedroom. A curtain suspended from a rail fitted to the ceiling serves as a dividing element.

© Catherine Tîg

© Catherine Tighe

337

© Rupert Stein

341

© José Luis Hausmann

■ The geometry inspired in the square-shaped windows has served as the creative theme for the interior design of this bedroom, from the chimney to the furniture and closets.

© Almond Ch

© Almond Chu

The bedroom is separated from the rest of the space by way of a glass partition and a dark colored heavy curtain, elements which allow various levels of integration.

© Jordi Miralles

© Jordi Miralles

© Paul Smoothy

351

© Trevor Me

© Jordi Miralli

the WilderNess geT LoSt.

© Volker Seding Photography

The latest industrial aesthetic is the source of inspiration for the layout of this bedroom, integrated with the social zone and bathroom on two of its sides.

357

359

© Adam Butler

© Elizabeth Felice

365

© Catherine Tighe

© Undine Pr

A longitudinal opening in the concrete wall creates an interesting visual connection between the bedroom and the staircase in this single-family residence.

© Jordi Miralle

■ The great height of this converted
industrial space has been fully
optimized to incorporate a metallic
structured mezzanine in which the
bedroom is housed.

© Jordi Miralle

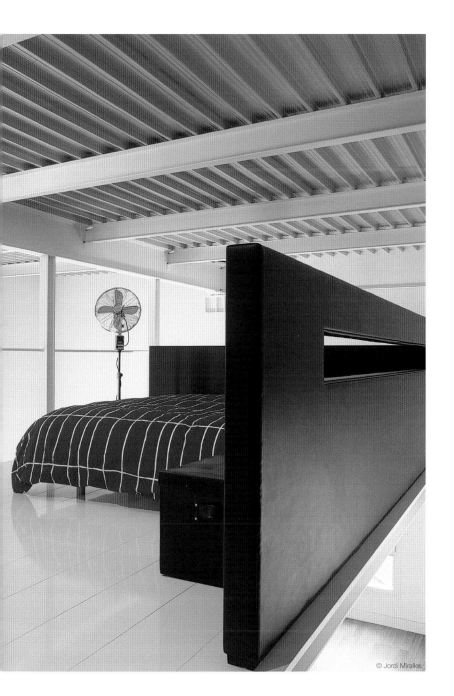

375

© Tony Miller

Concrete, metal, wood, and glass
have been carefully blended to create
a luminous and cozy ambience. An
interesting use of levels creates a
shelf unit concealed behind the
headboard of the bed.

© Yael Pinc

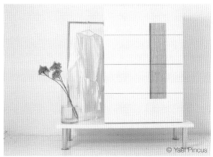

Large-scale glass partitions which extend from the floor to the ceiling, have been used to isolate the bedroom and also to give continuity to this former industrial space.

© Ignacio Martinez

© Rui Morais de Sous

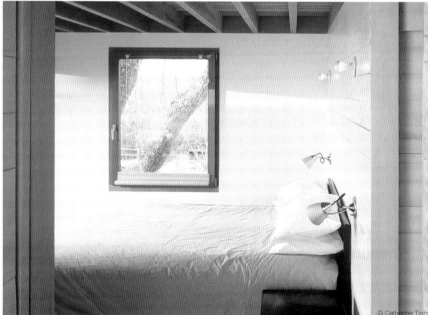

© Catherine Tigh

© Joan Roig

© Shania Sheged

Regardless of the type of house, wood
always plays a fundamental role in the
bedroom zone. It is a material that
adapts with ease to any style and
brings warmth to the space.

© Tim Griffith

Kids' Rooms

The kids' rooms are unique in that they are truly dynamic and multifunctional spaces. They are bedrooms with rest areas, but also studies with work and play zones. Such a variety of activities call for an intelligent and effective design that results in a space of contrasting and unique characteristics. It should be a cozy, fun space with a calm feel to it; utilize resistant, yet comfortable materials and finishes; and, above all, include a spacious area for playing, as well as plenty of storage space. Architects and designers need to unite these characteristics and create a uniform space, which on the one hand reflects the personalities of the kids, and on the other is functional and practical for adults. Flexibility, growth, and the changing tastes of the youngsters as time goes by are important considerations. In addition, the safety aspect, especially in the rooms of the very young ones, is paramount.

Depending on the ages of the children, as well as the parents' personal preferences, the interior design of these spaces can be very varied. Choices range from the rustic or more classic spaces to rooms that feature the latest technology, including electronic monitors for babies and the play area, as well as items such as computers for older children's study or work areas. Furniture is available that facilitates the layout of these rooms, or the component elements can be specifically designed for the space. Decoration in soft tones, like white, gray, or beige, is a more durable option, as brighter colors, although useful in creating a more personal and striking atmosphere, may need to be changed or modified over time.

With just a few pieces of furniture, wallpaper, and a bold choice of color, an attractive and cozy space with a personal touch can be achieved.

© J. J. Pérez Iscla

J. J. Pérez Iscla

401

© José Luis Hausmann

© José Luis Hausmann

© J. J. Pérez Iscla

Bunk beds, the ideal
traditional solution when
creating a room for two
children, contribute to
maximizing of the play
area space.

© J. J. Pérez [sc]

Furniture features, in this case the drawer handles, can serve as a focal point in creating an attractive and fun design element within a child's bedroom.

© J. J. Pérez Iscla

409

411

413

■ This interesting system of rails
attached to one of the bedroom
walls allows the beds to be
positioned differently, thus
creating a really flexible space.

© Dear

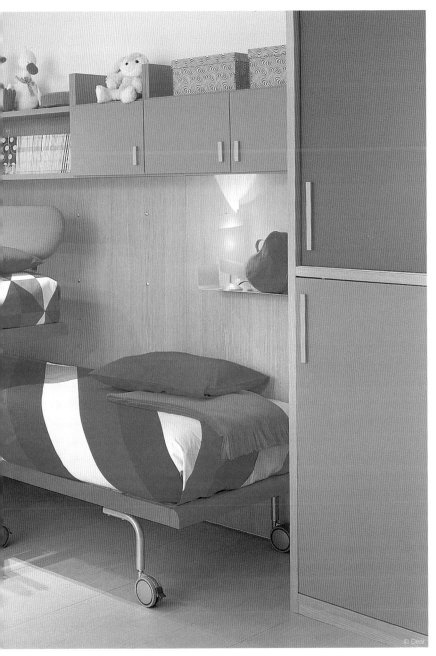

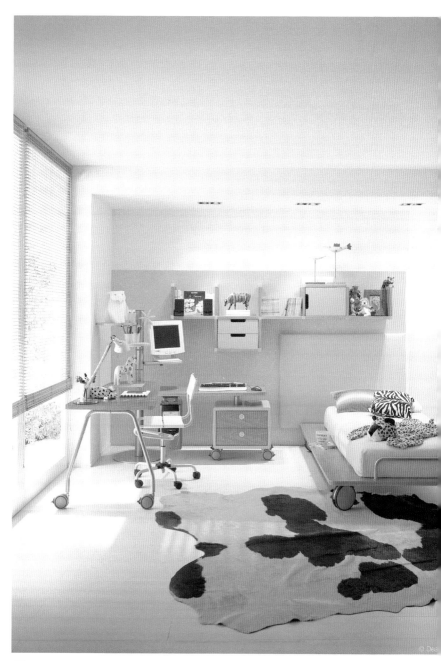

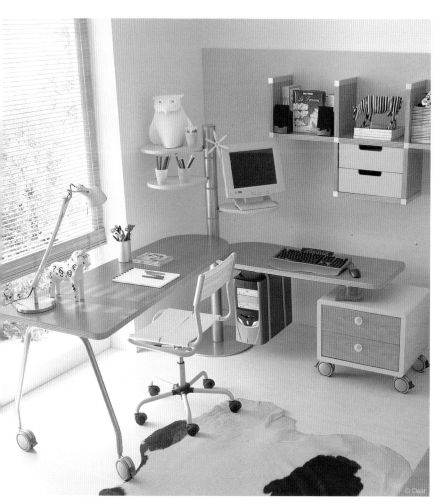

The corner piece of furniture in this
room rotates on the axis of a metallic
column that supports the diverse
work surfaces and shelves, which
can be rearranged as needed.

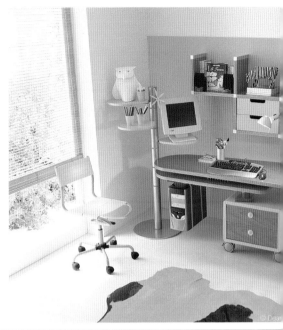

This piece of furniture attached to one of the walls of the room allows the work surfaces to be placed in front of each other or side by side, as desired.

© Jose Luis Hausmar

© Luis P

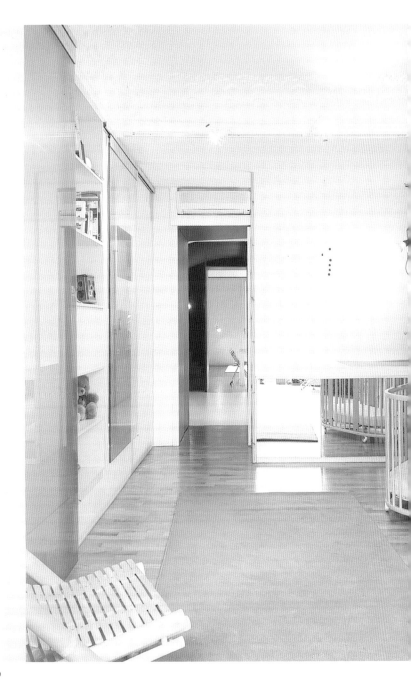

431

Light-colored pine adapts very well to the juvenile image of kids' rooms. Its light feel and malleability allow for the creation of various easily manipulated furniture elements.

© Kinder Räume

© Kinder Räume

© Leroa

435

© Tisettanta

437

© Tisettanta

© Tisettant

© Tisettanta

The wheels and the simple symmetrical
details of the headboard and the underside of
the bed allow for its transformation into a sofa,
thus creating a living zone during the day.

© José Luis Hausmar

© José Luis Hausman

© José Luis Hausmann

447

© Ricardo Labougle, Ana Cardinale

A high, deep design allows this
sofa to double up as a bed. Its
lower part serves as a storage
cupboard, using sliding drawers.

© Ricardo Labougle, Ana Cardinale

455

© Jordi Sarra

457

458

461

© Jordi Sarrà

© Jordi Sarrà

© Kinder Räume

464

Bathrooms

The bathroom, similar to the kitchen, is one of the spaces of the house that has undergone the most transformation in recent years as a result of the implementation of new technology, materials, and finishes. The design of the bathroom has always adapted to the habits and characteristics of each era. In the past, having a bath was something of a ritual that focused on worshipping the body, whether in the privacy of the home or in the social setting of a public bath. Despite the multiple transformations this space has experienced, the bathroom still preserves its special character within the house. Over time new water-resistant materials have been introduced, and bathrooms today are true sanctuaries for personal hygiene and relaxation. One of the essential requirements when designing a bathroom is to endow it with the maximum luminosity and spaciousness while conserving the desired intimacy.

The technical characteristics of the bathroom have repercussions as much on designs that use traditional materials, such as wood, glass, ceramics, or marble, as on those that specify innovative finishes, such as porcelain, resins, or stainless steel. Presently there are numerous style guides that allow the design of a classic or avant-garde bathroom with a rustic feel or stylized minimalist shapes. The lighting must allow for different levels of luminosity, from the very low subtle lighting, ideal for soaking in a relaxing bath, to the most homogeneous and intense for the area of the mirror. The influence of other cultures, such as the Scandinavian or Japanese, has contributed to this change in attitude with regard to the bathroom. This room is seen quite naturally as a room in which a positive state of mind is as important as body care. This concept has led to a blossoming bathroom culture that no longer simply views the room as a place to wash oneself, but rather as a space in which to relax and feel good.

471

473

The freestanding wall that separates the sink from the shower clearly defines these two zones; however, it also promotes fluidity within the space and accentuates the spaciousness.

© J. J. Pérez

The interesting geometric design of this bathroom is accentuated by an original mix of materials, textures, and colors that help to define each element within the space.

© J.J. Pelet...

479

© Eugeni Por

Glass has been used in this
bathroom to create the sink and
bath. The stainless steel features
and visible pipes highlight the
industrial character of the dwelling.

© Eugeni Pons

The absence of ceramic wall
coverings in this bathroom
space gives it the feel of a living
room. This effect is further
heightened by a curtain and
the graphic art on the walls.

489

491

© J. J. Pérez (sc)

© J. J. Pérez (sc)

© J. J. Pérez Iscla

White, the dominant feature in this ample space, serves as an ideal frame for highlighting the designer faucets and somber bathroom furniture.

© Paul Ott

© Ricardo Labougle, Ana Cardinale

498

© Rupert Steiner

In order to optimize the available space in this dwelling, the closets have been integrated into the bathroom zone. The translucent glass partitions serve as dividing elements.

© Rupert Steiner

© Hans Peter Wörnd

Birch plywood panels have been used to fashion diverse cupboards and to create an interestingly spacious layout in the interior of this bathroom.

© Hans Peter Wörnd

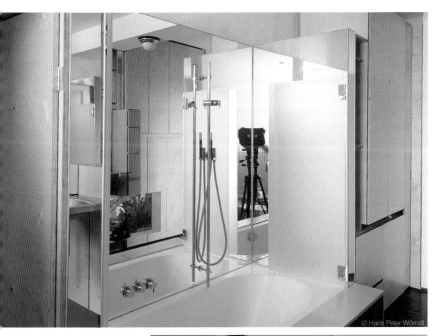

© Hans Peter Wörndl

509

© Nuria Fuente

511

© Nuria Fuente

© Nuria Fuentes

© Adam Butler

The sobriety of this space reserved
exclusively for the bath is achieved
by way of indirect lighting and the
opaque glass paneling that
surrounds the space.

© Adam Butler

519

© J. J. Pérez Iscle

© Lichtblau Wagner Architekten

© Lichtblau Wagner Architekten

The elegance of this bathroom is achieved by using minimalist elements that highlight the contrast between the white of the fixtures and the black used in some of the surfaces.

© Flaminia

© Flaminia

© Flaminia

The use of polished cement for the floor and wall coverings in this bath zone provides an interesting alternative to the traditional ceramics.

© Virginia Del Guidice

© Virginia Del Guidice

527

© Werner Huthmacher

In conversions of old industrial warehouses, an open-plan bathroom helps accentuate the diaphanous character of this type of space.

© Werner Huthmacher

531

© Rupert Steiner

533

Reminders of the baroque style,
apparent in the marble coverings,
mirrors, and decorative details,
contrast with the avant-garde style
of the bathroom fixtures.

© Duravit

© Duravi

© Duravit

© Duravit

© Durav

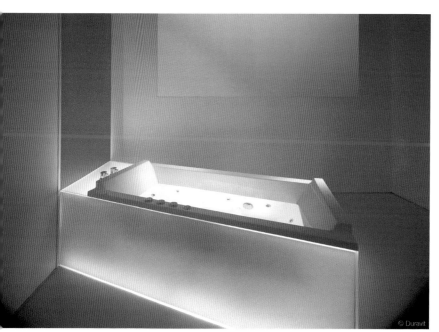

© Duravit

The polycarbonate covering of the bathtub serves to create an interesting light box within this space, complete with rectangular shapes and intense colors.

© Adam Butler

This bathroom is divided into three zones: the shower, completely fitted with limestone walls; a small closed room for the toilet; and sink space that opens onto the courtyard.

© Adam Butler

© Duravit

© Duravit

© Tony Miller

© Tony Miller

grand have *made*
sing long many

alphabet anchor answered
common delight devise

prepare quarrel real
vanish wonder rate

© Werner Huthmacher

© Arnaldo Pappalardo

© Eugeni Pons

© Eugeni Pons

© Paul Warchol

© Paul Warchol

© Paul Warchol

Novel materials such as
enameled cement or
glass offer attractive and
contemporary alternatives
for the covering of the
surfaces of the bathroom.

© Shania Shegedyn

565

Work Spaces

The idea of working from home is today a relatively common concept. Even those who don't work professionally from home usually reserve some corner of the house for computer work space or a desk. From the early 20th century, when bohemian artists lived in their own workshops, people of varying professions have continued to incorporate workplaces into their homes. For artists, the considerations were both physical and economical: they could work at odd hours, when inspiration struck, while also avoiding the expense of maintaining a separate work space. Nowadays the reasons have multiplied. While towns grew, so did the distances between the office and the home, which meant commuting times were longer and less pleasant. Furthermore, the eight-hour workday became less compatible with housework, as well as a limitation for those who did extra work in the afternoons or evenings. Gradually, working from home has been converted into a chance to create an intimate and personalized ambience that results in a familiar, economical, and comfortable place to work.

However, the most crucial aspect of this revolution has been, without a doubt, the boom in information technology and its impact on work. People can travel today without leaving the house, and enormous amounts of information can be compiled and sent in just a few seconds by simply pressing some keys. The concept of working independently has been given a great impetus, thus promoting the idea of creating an office at home. The advantages include having a flexible timetable, along with an aesthetically pleasing and comfortable work space. The design of the illumination is important and direct sunlight should be avoided. Depending on the type of work and the number of workers, it is usually preferable to make this area as independent as possible in relation to the rest of the house.

In an open and diaphanous loft-type space, a work zone is achieved through simply placing a table in a well-illuminated corner of the area.

© Wini Sulzbach

© Eugeni Pons

© Eugeni Pons

© Eugeni Pons

© Eugeni Pons

© Werner Huthmacher

© Werner Hutchmacher

The thin shelving units serve as a showcase for the books, which are the main feature of this studio. The large space can be divided into smaller meeting rooms by the sliding doors.

© Alessandro Ciampi

583

A longitudinal table that serves as a work zone has been fitted to one of the walls of this large-sized room.

587

© Eugeni Pons

© Chris Tubbs

589

© Chris Tubbs

The office is concealed behind
the folding doors, which can
completely transform this small
space into a living area or a
working zone.

© Chris Tubbs

© Paul Ott

595

© Nuria Fuentes

© Nuria Fuentes

The design of the furniture is fundamental for the maximum efficiency of an office at home, especially when endeavoring to get the most out of the available space.

© Nuria Fuentes

© Nuria Fuentes

A shelf was positioned under the large work surface to avoid detracting from the distinctive stone walls.

604

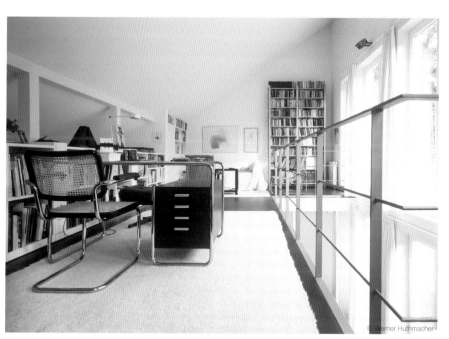

The former attic of this house was altered to create a large work area. The structure of the roof itself brings real character to the space.

The layout of the furniture in this
small-sized apartment enables the
space to be used as a bedroom,
living room, dining room, or study,
as desired.

© Eugeni Pons

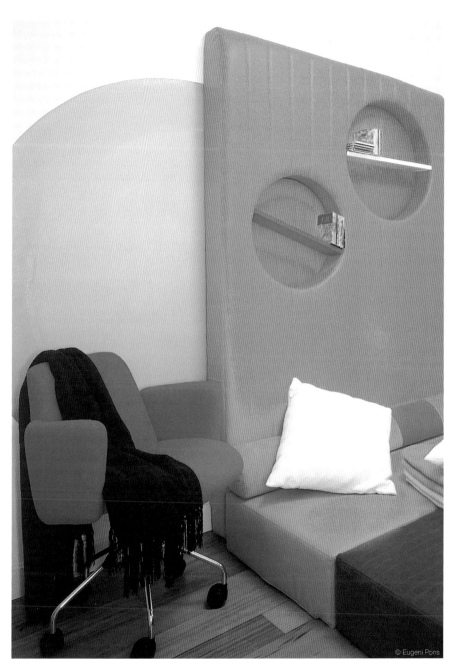

© Eugeni Pons

© Alessandro Ciampi

© Alessandro Campi

623

© Adolf Bereuter

The cleanness of this space, which has been achieved through the uniformity of color and the texture of the surfaces, gives center stage to the work furniture contained herein.

© Eugeni Pons

© Eugeni Pons

■ In this loft, the office space is concealed
behind a practical lightweight screen
that features metallic edges and
polycarbonate panels through which
the light can flow.

© Jordi Miralles

629

© Tisettanta

This sizable shelving unit in
the living room of the house is
transformed into an office by
simply folding back the wooden
doors concealing the computer.